C000185649

The Burnhams
People & Places

A photographic portrait of the seven Norfolk villages
at the end of the first decade of the twenty-first century

Hazel Denslow & John Warham

Dedication

To Sue and Evelyn

Debbie, Jane and Geoff

First Published 2012

ISBN 978-0-9553333-5-4

A catalogue record for this book is available from the British Library.

Designed by Dick Malt

Published by Thornham Local History Society
Red Brick House
Hall Lane
Thornham
Norfolk PE36 6NB

Printed by Dolphin Graphics
Dersingham, Norfolk

Contents

Introduction

The Burnhams – People & Places, is the third in a series of photographic books portraying the villages and towns of the north Norfolk coast. Like its predecessors, *Thornham – People & Places* and *Wells-next-the-Sea – People & Places*, it is an attempt to capture the character and spirit of the Burnhams at a specific point in time – the end of the first decade of the twenty-first century. 'Change is the only constant' is a mantra which applies as much to this quiet corner as it does to anywhere else. Looking back, I am amazed at how much has changed in Thornham and Wells in the short time since those books were published. While working on this book, we have seen the Jockey re-open as the Nelson, Barclays Bank has closed its doors and the summer traffic in Burnham Market just gets worse! The choice of the Burnhams as a holiday and second-home destination shows no sign of slacking.

In attempting a portrait of the Burnhams, I faced the same problem as with the Wells book; by now, I knew the format worked, but lacked the local contact who knew the local residents and could persuade them to take part. This time, I had the good fortune to team up with Hazel Denslow, a fellow student for many years at what is becoming known amongst its followers as the 'Julia Rafferty School of Photography' at Wells Library. Hazel has lived in Burnham Market since 1993 and added the extra dimension in persuading the local characters, trades people and shop keepers to stand still long enough to be captured on camera. We are especially grateful to the people in the Burnhams who good-humouredly allowed us to intrude our lenses briefly into their daily lives.

Raymond Monbiot and The Burnhams Society History Group, who produced the *Photographic History of the Burnhams*, published by Halsgrove Press, also helped us by providing the background to the development and changes to the Burnham villages over the centuries. With their permission, we have used some old photographs, where appropriate, to illustrate the backcloth against which the Burnhams now stand.

Burnham Market

There were once seven Burnhams by the Sea. Westgate, Sutton and Ulph were amalgamated into Burnham Market during the nineteenth century, leaving Burnham Deepdale, Market, Norton, Overy Staithe, Overy Town and Thorpe.

A panoramic view of the Market Place from Burnham Westgate church.

The Market Place

A sample of the many shops and fine Georgian buildings on and around the market square.

PAMELA NOYES
Paintings

Lime Green

GUN HILL

Grooms
BAKERY

ST. EDMUNDS

DTZ
For Sale
0115 901
5150
BARCLAYS

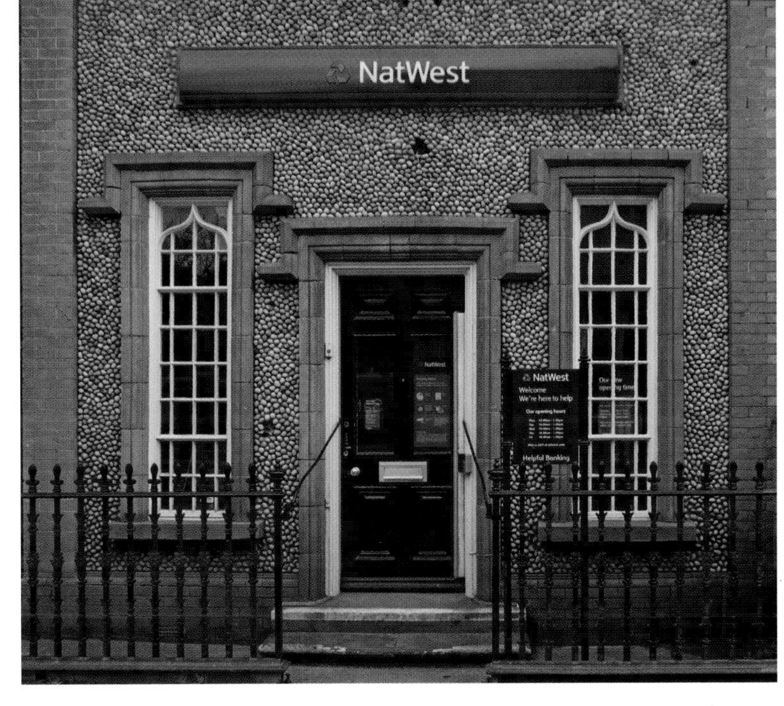
NatWest
NatWest
Welcome
We're here to help
Our opening hours
Helpful Banking

Burnham Westgate Hall

Built in the 1750s and extensively rebuilt by the famous Georgian architect Sir John Soane in the 1780s, Westgate Hall has had a varied history. Originally a country house, it was donated to the Royal British Legion, served as an old people's home and eventually reverted to private ownership. The Hall was put up for sale again in 2011.

NORFOLK LIVING

GURNEYS FISH SHOP
LEMON SOLE - COD - MONK
WILD SEA BASS - BRILL
DOVER SOLE - HALIBUT
LOCAL CRAB
BRILL
GURNEYS
FISH
SHOP
OPEN
LOBSTER
TODAY

Lucy's
Outstanding Cakes
Fine Food,
Teas & Coffee
Lucy's
Outstanding Cakes, Fine Food
Teas & Coffee

The Brazen Head Bookshop and Gallery
CLOSED

UTTINGS

Norfolk Green
hopper

BUTCHER
HOWELL

Christmas

The lights go up and Susan Riseborough is out in her Mrs Christmas outfit, selling tickets for the 'Children in Need' raffle. On Christmas Day the village is quiet for once in the year.

THE
HOSTE
ARMS
17th CENTURY
COACHING INN
35 Bedrooms
www.hostearms.co.uk

TELEPHONE

Well-known local photographer Harry Cory-Wright with his daughters Katherine & Mary.

Not a regular event in these times of drier and milder winters, but this part of Norfolk does get its fair share of snow on occasions.

St Mary's Church, Burnham Westgate

Now the main parish church, St Mary's stands in a classic, imposing position at the west end of the village looking down to the market place. The interesting frieze on the tower depicts events from the Bible. It was probably a bequest from William Lexham, Lord of the Manor in 1500.

Palm Sunday

Rev. Graham Hitchins and David Crombie, lay minister and former co-owner of the White House bookshop.

St Henry's Roman Catholic Church

Burnham Market's Catholic Church is named after the Jesuit priest and martyr, Henry Walpole, a Norfolk man born in Docking in 1558.

Walpole followed in the footsteps of other English martyrs such as Edmund Campion, studying at the English College in Rome before being sent to England where he was captured, imprisoned in the Tower and executed in York.

Methodist Church

The Methodist Church on Station Road was previously a Salvation Army Tabernacle built in 1920. The old chapel fell into disrepair and, after much fund-raising, was replaced in 1994. The chapel hosts Wells Sure Start Toddlers' Group and the local Youth Club.

Rev. Kim Nally is the minister.

Gospel Hall

In times gone by, the Gospel Hall was a thriving community, with a Sunday school attended by many children, and organised outings. Now, in common with many other places of worship, the congregation is sadly diminished.

Dorothy Smith is the organist.

Saint Ethelbert's Church, Burnham Sutton

Not much remains of the old Saxon church named after Ethelbert, an eighth-century king of East Anglia. The walls of the nave and tower were excavated by the Burnham Market Society in the 1990s.

All Saints' Church, Burnham Sutton cum Ulph

All Saints' Church is possibly the earliest of Burnham Market's churches and stands at the opposite end of the village from St Mary's, Westgate. When St Ethelbert's Church in Burnham Sutton fell into disrepair, some of the building materials were moved and used to renovate All Saints. The two parishes have officially been known as All Saints', Burnham Sutton cum Ulph, since 1772.

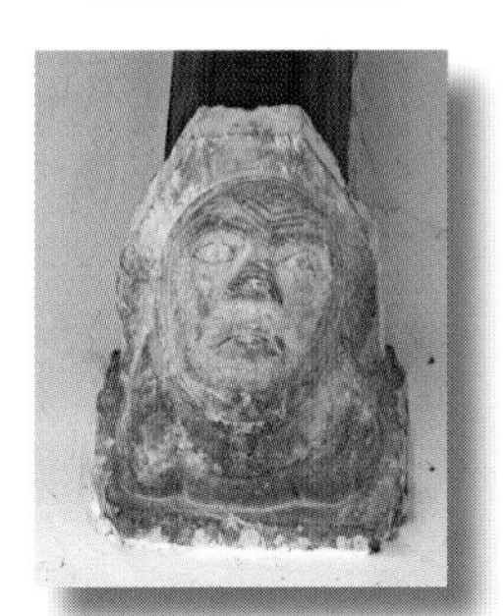

BIBLE

The Carmelite Friary

From the time of the biblical prophet Elijah, there had been Holy Hermits on Mount Carmel in Palestine. In 1237 their prior was an Englishman called Simon; probably the man known today as Saint Simon Stock. He had to evacuate his brethren because of the Crusades, and one of the first places the Carmelite friars landed was north Norfolk. In 1241 Ralph Hempnale and Sir William Calthorp founded a house of Whitefriars at Bradmer, a site east of Burnham Norton. Within a decade it had moved to the present site, perhaps because of the water supply. The friary was enlarged in 1298 and in 1353, which is probably the date of the gatehouse shown above.

This remote friary housed up to twelve men and lasted 300 years, during which time the Whitefriars expanded all over England with famous teaching houses at Oxford and Cambridge. Their Burnham house seems to have remained as a retreat to remind them of their origins. Their most famous prior was Robert Bale who was buried here in 1503. Many locals left bequests to the Burnham Whitefriars right up to the dissolution of the monasteries. The site was sold to the Calthorpes and later to the Pepys family, relatives of the London diarist.

Burnham Market Traffic

Burnham Market is notorious for traffic during the summer months. It certainly comes in a great variety of ways throughout the year, as these photos show.

NON HAZARDOUS
PRODUCT
KP53 OTC
C156
BURNHAM MARKET
PLEASE
DRIVE SLOWLY
NORFOLK C.C.

Lucy's

The war memorial was unveiled in 1920. The names of those killed in the Second World War were added in a dedication service in 1947.

When the water table is high, the Goosebeck, which rises in a spring in the grounds of Westgate Hall, flows through the market place. It crosses the road in the centre before disappearing into a culvert which discharges into the Burn.

Left
Spring cleaning.

Front Street

When this old photograph was taken, most of the buildings on Front Street were shops, almost none of which have survived to the present day. Most have been converted into holiday accommodation.

Steve, Sheila & Tony Green

Overy Road, Ulph Place

Burnham Market Craft Fair

This has been a popular annual event since 1976 and features stalls set out on the green selling handmade crafts from around the area. The parish council distributes the proceeds to the school and other organisations in the Burnhams.

LITTLE
ACORNS
LEMON
G&T
CHILLI
GARLIC
COURGETTE PEAS CURLY KALE

*Book Sale
Hardbacks £4.00
Paperbacks £1.50

Jenny Rose (above left), Julie and Rob King (above), Ellie Beachell and Rob Rutterford (below).

AO59 PXR

Punch & Judy

Burnham Market Auctions

Every Monday afternoon in the summer holidays, auctions take place on Fairstead Green, next to Westgate church, just as they have done in Burnham Market for centuries.

Until his death in 2008, auctions were run by John Dewing of Case & Dewing.

The current auctioneer is Geoff Misson, ably assisted by the cashier Terry Rand.

The Burnhams Flower Show and Carnival

The Flower Show, organised by the Horticultural Society, was started in 1903 and takes place on the playing field. Floats assemble in front of Westgate Church and make their way to the field where competitions, including the slow bicycle race, take place. On this occasion, music was provided by the Next Generation Steel Band.

Bayer Garden
We can help
Bayer Garden
Bayer Garden
Bayer Garden
We can help
phostrogen

FUNFAIR
ALL RIDES ONLY £1 THURSDAY
BURNHAM MARKET
PLAYING FIELD
Thur 7th July 6.30 - late
Fri 8th July 6.30 - late
Sat 9th July 1.00 - late
SUN 10th July 12-00 - 6-00
Telephone: 07771 620126 Temporary Notice: This poster will be removed after the event

THIS SATURDAY
9th JULY
1-45 to 2-00pm
EXPECT DELAYS
AND
TEMPORARY ROAD
CLOSURERS HERE
BURNHAM MARKET CARNIVAL

FLYING SAUCER

CATCH A CHARACTER TO WIN
A PRIZE EVERY TIME
CATCH A CHARACTER TO WIN
A PRIZE EVERY TIME

Princess

John Sower, Joan Rix, Steve Evans, Caroline Hill, Claire Butcher, James Pollock, Victoria Bennett, Bill Offord, Kevin Skinner, Brian Rix, Peter Groom, Veronica Groom, Janet Offord and Hazel Denslow.

Tennis Club

Burnham Market has an active tennis club. It was founded in 1989 with money raised by local fund-raising and regional and national grant awards. The club has developed over the years with the installation of floodlights. Children are encouraged to join and are offered free coaching sessions.

Burnham Market Horse Trials

Started in 1999, Burnham Market Horse Trials is now one of the country's leading equestrian events. It is also a great day out with plenty of stands and activities for all the family.

The Round Norfolk Relay

The Round Norfolk Relay, sponsored by Birkett's, attracts runners from all over Europe. Teams of seventeen complete a gruelling course of 194 miles around Norfolk, non-stop, over two days, starting and finishing in King's Lynn. Stage three comes through Burnham Overy Staithe from Hunstanton for the run to Wells.

Cycle Tour of Britain

The Tour of Britain is the UK's biggest professional bicycle race and was previously known as the Milk Race, the Kellogg's Tour of Britain and the PruTour. Stage Six of the 2010 race started in King's Lynn and passed through Burnham Market before ending 118 miles later, in Great Yarmouth.

The Hoste Arms

The Hoste Arms started life as an unassuming pub, the Pitt Arms, in 1700, named after Thomas Pitt who owned Westgate Hall. It was renamed Sir William Hoste Arms in 1811 after the captain who served under Nelson in the Napoleonic Wars. Now it is a well-known hotel and restaurant, built up by the late Paul Whittome and his wife Jeanne.

TELEPHONE

TRANQUIL GARDEN

Nicki Grey, Claire Hubbard, Beth Lombari
and Denise Legallez.

Super Car Rally

The Hoste Arms Supercar Rally was started by Paul Whittome in 2010 and attracts an array of star marques as well as star personalities. John Lennon's Mercedes limosine was a favourite in the 2010 show.

Middle right
Jeanne Whittome and Sarah Eddison.

The Nelson

Originally the Mermaid, later the Lord Nelson and, more recently, the Jockey, the pub was taken over by Andrew Waddison in 2011 and renamed the Nelson, thereby restoring the local connection.

The pub suffered serious bomb damage in 1942 and the differences can be seen in these photos.

The Surgery

When opened 1981, the Surgery received a commendation from the Civic Trust for, 'its contribution to the quality and appearance of the environment'.

The School

The present school building opened in 1954 and now serves as a primary school for many of the surrounding villages whose schools have closed down over the years.

Post Office, Post Ladies

Dianne Eastwood behind the counter in the post office.

Post ladies Teresa Mahon and Sue Arnold have been delivering the mail for eighteen and twenty-five years respectively.

Pamela Noyes

Pamela was born and brought up in north Norfolk and has been painting East Anglian landscapes for many years. She specialises in oils and is well known for her large canvases of Holkham beach, cattle on the marshes and vibrant still-life paintings.

Andrew Ruffhead

Andrew Ruffhead retired to Burnham Market in 2006 after a career in textile design. His small studio is a splash of vivid colour featuring different types of recycled flotsam and jetsam from local beaches. Andrew collects all types of interesting pieces during his beachcombing, which he turns into colourful lobsters and smiling fish – there is has a touch of quirkiness about much of his work. Andrew describes himself as, 'passionate about using what others would consider as rubbish or waste and making something new out of them. It is fun to create my artworks out of something which was totally different in a former life'. Specially commissioned maps of the coast full of humorous illustrations are also one of his specialities. His largest map to date is six feet wide and covers the coast from Thornham to Salthouse. As well as being featured widely in local shops, Andrew's pieces are found as far away as Greece and Australia.

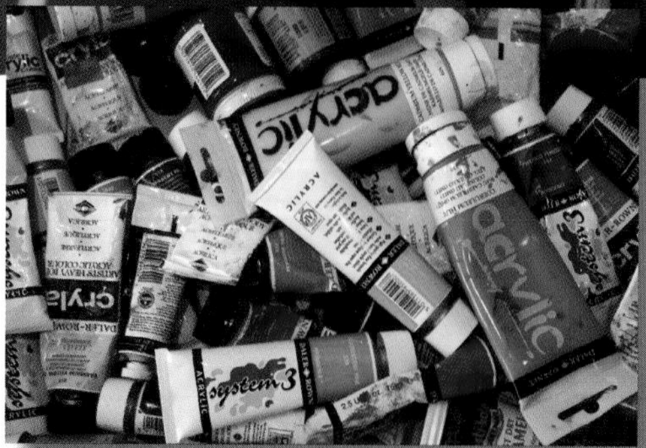

Bloomin'Gorgeous

Andrea St Quintin moved her florist business from Burnham Deepdale to Ulph Place in 2010. As well as offering fresh-cut flowers and bouquets, Andrea has a workshop and coffee shop for customers to relax in and watch her at work.

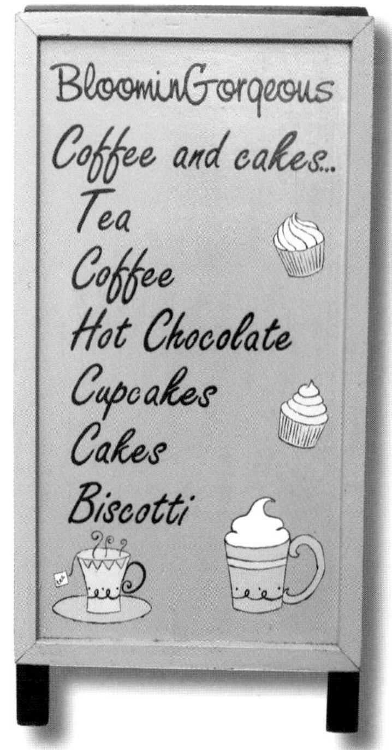

Groom's Bakery

There has been a bakery here since 1923. James Groom, the current baker, is the fourth generation to bake in Burnham Market.

Fredz

Joanna Warner, a hairdresser for twenty-seven years, took over the Hairdressers in Burnham Market in 2009. Jo named the shop after her daughter Frederika who also works in the business. Fredz pride themselves on being a friendly team offering a warm welcome to all. Fiona Farrow, Nicky Bond and Anna Holman are the other members of the team.

Gun Hill

Nick Fryer enjoyed many childhood holidays on the Norfolk coast before moving to Burnham Market in 1994 to open 'Gun Hill'. The original premises were on Overy Road and moved to Clifton House, in the Market Square, in 2002. The building was a butcher's shop between the wars and was then used by the Home Guard during the Second World War before reverting to a private house. It now stocks both ladies' and men's casual clothing. All the clothing is chosen by Nick and his wife Lucy to provide everything needed for a weekend on the coast, from walking on the beach to enjoying a drink in the pub or eating out with friends.

Ned Catt, Alastair Steele, Matthew Falvey and (below) Mike Gurney

Gurneys

Mike Gurney worked as a warden for the National Trust at Brancaster before starting to smoke fish for Fishes Restaurant. Then, in 1976, he went on to open his own small business, in Brancaster. In 1992 he opened Gurneys in Burnham Market and sources as much local produce as possible.

Arthur Howell

Arthur Howell's great-grandfather, also Arthur, opened his first shop, still trading today, in Binham in 1889. Howell's also operates two other shops in Wells. (Right) Brian Hetherington

Humble Pie

In earlier times these premises have been an outfitter's, hairdresser's, tobacconist's, confectioner's and butcher's shop. Now owned by Sue Elston (below) who has run Humble Pie since 1980.

Ben Andrews, Sam Turner and Beverley Defew

Janet Betts

Church Walk Florist, run by husband and wife Keith and Janet Betts, was established in 1990, selling locally grown bunches of flowers. The business grew into a very well stocked florist with fresh flowers being delivered three or four times a week. Sadly the business closed at the end of 2011 because of ill health.

Pentney House

Over twenty-five years ago, Pentney House was let as a holiday cottage by Gloria Hurn (right). She then began to sell china, bric-a-brac, bits of furniture and hats, laying the latter out on beds. From this small beginning, the family business has grown and now has what is claimed to be the biggest selection of hats in the country.

Ann Randall (far left), Debbie Lawton and Sophie Smith

Sands Pharmacy

Dating from around 1700, the building first became a pharmacy in 1835 when Henry Nash bought the property. Since then, there have been eight pharmacists. Brian Symonds is the present owner and has run the business for the past twenty years. In 1835, a local man was poisoned by his wife and her accomplice, who collaborated to buy arsenic from the pharmacy. The two women were publicly hanged in Norwich.

Above
Lynn Hinson, Karen Cole, Sally Wordingham and Brian Symonds

Satchells

Maxwell Graham-Wood picked up an early interest in wine from his father and travelled around France for two years after leaving school, working in the major wine-producing areas and learning the trade. He has been running the Satchells business since 1990.

This former chapel was home to Congregationalists, Quakers and Methodists, as well as being an iron foundry, iron-mongers and a wine and spirit merchant. For a few years, Sally Whitworth ran the shop known as 'Treasure Island' from here.

Urban Armour

Urban Armour was established more than twenty years ago and relocated to Burnham Market in 2003. Owned by Charles and Brygida Bourn, the shop specialises in contemporary and fashionable sterling silver jewellery.

Uttings

Ernest (Ernie) Utting opened a shop in the early thirties in North Street. Following war service in the RAF, he re-opened his business in Front Street, moving into the current premises on the Green in 1953. His son Alan took over in 1976, passing the business on to his children Richard and Victoria in 2010. Uttings started by selling TV and radio, then hardware and white goods. The shop now sells kitchenware, hardware, fruit and vegetables. Debbie Davies is behind the counter.

Whitehouse Books

Whitehouse Books has been in business for some sixteen years. The owner, Catherine Bennett (Kate to most people) took over the shop in November 2007 having retired from her solicitor's practice and moved to Norfolk. People often ask her whether she really enjoys running a bookshop. Doesn't she miss being a solicitor? Her answers are always the same: 'Yes', and 'No'. Almost since she left school Catherine has dreamed of having her own bookshop.

BKidZ

Annie Gordon trained at Chelsea School of Art and then ran an interior design business. Following the arrival of grandchildren she changed direction, opening the BKidZ toyshop in Emma's Court.

burnham
grapevine
CONTEMPORARY ARTS

Burnham
Interiors
Tel: 01328 730989

GILLY'S
of
BURNHAM MARKET
LADIES
FASHIONS

Lucy's
Outstanding Cakes
Fine Food
Teas & Coffee
01328 730908

Ruby and
Tallulah
BOUTIQUE
01328 738638

ANNA
BURNHAM MARKET
PRIMROSE HILL
KINGS ROAD
BURY ST EDMUNDS
SAFFRON WALDEN
HARPENDEN

JACK
WILLS
London England
OUTFITTERS
TO THE
GENTRY

M&A CRINGLE
CLOSED

HAMILTON
ANTIQUES

STORM
FINE ART

THE WAREHO S

Lime Green

TILLY'S
CAFE
CAFE

Norfolk
Country
Cottages

Abbotts

Bedfords
est.1966

SOWERBYS

shoes
on the
green

BURNHAM MARKET
POST
OFFICE

FAIRFAX
GALLERY

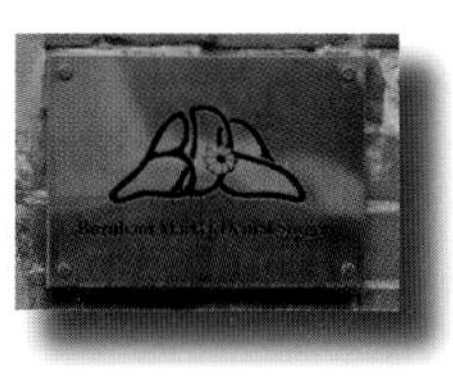

BRUCE
& COMPANY

SILK ROAD
Authentic Peking & Cantonese Takeaway

the
artmonger
01328 730370

CLASSIC
SHEDS

BURNHAM MARKET PINE
FURNITURE

JOULES
ESTABLISHED IN THE FIELDS OF GREAT BRITAIN

NORFOLK LIVING

The Mermaid
Traditional Fish & Chips

Catherine Alexandra

Burnham Market Stores

Corner House
BOUTIQUE SALON
3

The Brazen Head Bookshop and Gallery
CLOSED

Tradesmen

Right, top row
James Granger; Trevor Manning; Brian Rix.

middle row
Steven Willsher; Kenny Thompson, Sean Allen, Martin Flowerdew & Simon Rix, (M & M); Nod Butcher (Nod-a-job).

bottom row
Gary Robins; Chris Geering; Dave, Bob & Jack Smith

Bright Spark

Born and bred in Burnham Norton, Jo Francis started her own business fifteen years ago, with help from the Prince's Trust. The cherry picker enables her to reach places others cannot reach.

Painting & Decorating

TREVOR MANNING

www.brianrix-builders.co.uk
NHBC
Burnham Market
Brian Rix
Builder
RI XYY

STEVEN WILLSHER
BUILDER & DECORATOR
BURNHAM MARKET
01328 738651
07876633074

M&M
Tel / Fax
NHBC
ZURICH

NOD-A-JOB
Burnham Market
General Maintenance
NOD BUTCHER
Builder of Burnham Market
All Types of Building Work
Painting & Decorating
FREE Estimate & Advice
Tel 01328 738754
Mob077764 11116
E-mail nod-a-job@hotmail.com
Experience

G. ROBINS
General Builder
Burnham Overy Staithe (01328) 738
Mobile: (07766) 952332

NHBC
R. M. SMITH
(Builders) LTD
BURNHAM MARKET
TEL: 01328 738519

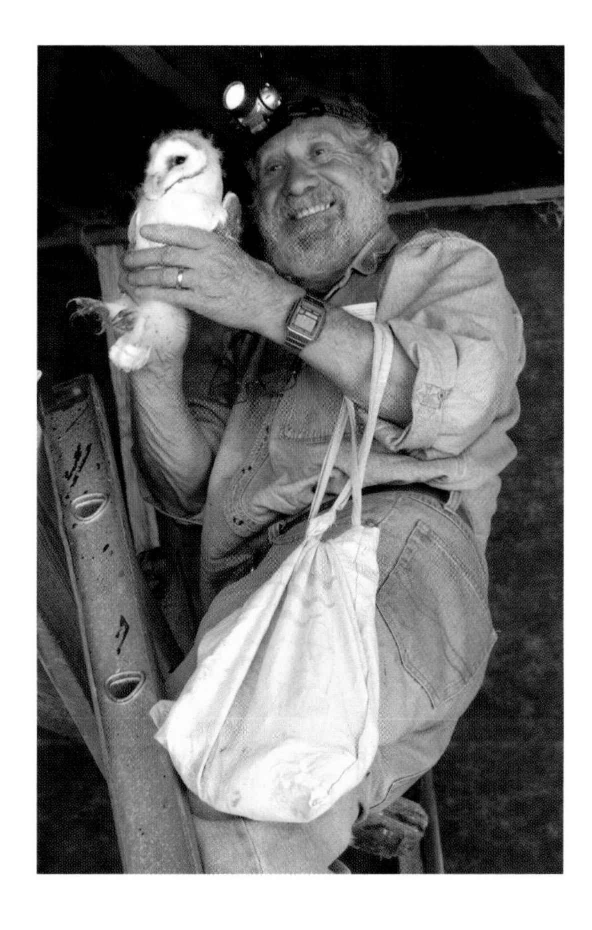

John Middleton

John Middleton has always been interested in bird migration and qualified as a ringer before becoming a co-founder of the North West Norfolk Ringing Group. Latterly, John has concentrated on barn owls. He once had the amazing experience of recovering a sand martin in Senegal – 6,000 miles from where he had ringed it in Norfolk!

Station Garage

The last remaining garage in Burnham Market – there used to be three – Station Garage on Creake Road provides motorists with full servicing, repair facilities and fuel, as well as provisions from the shop.

From top
Scott Raven, Robert Harker and Kevin Hewitt

The Old Railway Station

The last passenger train left Burnham Market station in 1952. The old railway station is now a bed and breakfast annexe of the Hoste Arms.

BEWARE
OF
TRAINS

GREAT WESTERN RAILWAY.
NOTICE IS HEREBY GIVEN
IN PURSUANCE OF THE PROVISIONS OF
SECTION 65 OF THE GREAT WESTERN RAILWAY
(ADDITIONAL POWERS) ACT, 1924, THAT
THIS IS A
PRIVATE ROAD

ANY PERSON WHO OMITS TO SHUT AND FASTEN THIS GATE
IS LIABLE TO A PENALTY NOT EXCEEDING FORTY SHILLINGS

Westgate Allotments

Sabine Schmitt, Brian Lynn, Ivan Sands, Charlie Neale.

Many of the allotments in England have their origins in the Enclosure Acts of the late eighteenth century. Westgate Allotments are rented from the Roy family by Burnham Market Parish Council.

For thirty-eight years, Brian Lynn has been working the same plot that his grandfather and great-grandfather worked. Brian says that renting allotments went out of fashion in the 1970s and many plots were left empty. With the advent of organic farming and local sourcing, the use of allotments is once more back in vogue.

Burnham Overy Staithe

Formerly the major port of the Burnhams, where supplies of coal and grain were offloaded before the advent of the railways, Overy Staithe is now a popular tourist destination and an active sailing centre with its summer regatta and water sports events.

BURNHAM OVERY STAITHE

One way

30

The Maltings was formerly the Moorings Hotel, established by George Phillips in 1926. It closed in 1979.

Captain
Richard Woodget
Master of the Cutty Sark
lived here
1899 – 1926

Burnham Overy
Town

Burnham Overy
Village Hall

Burnham Overy
Parish Council

GONG LANE

The Hero
Burnham Overy Staithe

HAVEN END

PLEASE LEAVE
TUBE ROUND
BACK.
THANKS.

ALLOTMENT
HOLDERS ONLY.
NO RABBITS!

Coasthopper
.co.uk
Coasthugging
you're never very far from
days a year on Coasthopper,
perfect for getting away from
the rat race (and the driving!)
Coasthopper
301
Bus Stop
Burnham Overy
Tower Road opp
The Hero
Coasthopper
traveline
Norfolk County Council
at your service
txt NFOAGPJP to 84268

Overy Staithe Fête

In its early days, the fête was held in various village gardens, particularly Judge Head's. It later moved to the local playing field and then to its present venue on John Atkinson's field. The small field gives a busy, intimate atmosphere and contributes to the success of this popular event held at the end of August each year. Children are fascinated by the hurdy-gurdy which is driven over from Thursford. Many of the thirty stalls are run by children themselves.

2
2
4
6

How many
blades of
Marram-grass
in this bundle ?
1 guess 20p
3 guesses 50p
Answer - Announcement with raffle.
Prize for winning guess and runner up.
Please collect from Boathouse if not received today at Fête.

Overy Staithe Harbour

The harbour and marshes of Burnham Overy Staithe are renowned for their natural beauty. The Burnham Overy Harbour Trust was formed in 1983 to protect this heritage site. The land is leased the from Holkham Estate.

Scolt Head Ferry

Transport by DUKW was one way to get out to Gun Hill and Scolt Head Island in the old days. There has also been a ferry taking out people and supplies since the 1930s. Peter Bickell now runs a summer service out to the island.

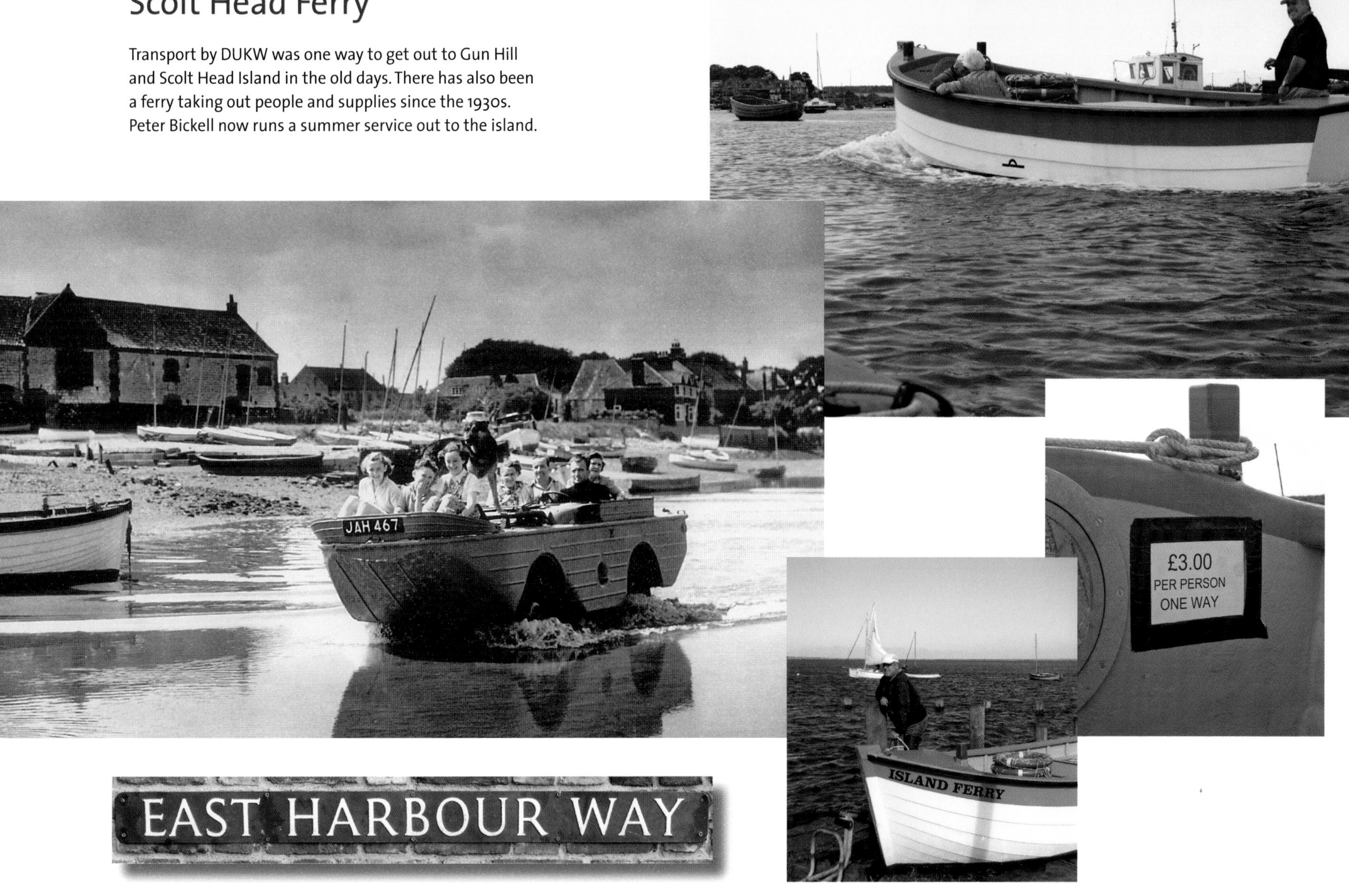

NO PARKING
ON JETTY
OR·IN
FRONT OF
SLIPWAY.
THANK YOU

WARNING
BATHING IS
DANGEROUS DURING
FLOOD & EBB
TIDES

At low tide the harbour is shallow enough to wade across, but high tides can catch out unwary motorists.

Juliette Short's ice cream van has become an institution at Overy Staithe. Every summer for the past twenty-nine years, Juliette has been selling ice cream on the Staithe, following in the footsteps of her father 'Jordi' who set up the business in the 1970s.

Crabbing or 'gillying' on the quayside.

The Boathouse

The Boathouse, run by Mick and Carole Coutanche, is a traditional chandlery offering boat storage, boat repairs and sailing gear.

The Boathouse features a webcam from which there is a constant view of the changing tides and a north-easterly view of the salt marshes with the sand dunes of Gun Hill in the distance.

Mick & Carole Coutanche, Pam Thompson

Peter Beck

Peter was born in Burnham Market and has lived in the Burnhams ever since, apart from his Navy years. Joining up at sixteen, he spent four years as an apprentice shipwright. After another four years he left the Navy to come back to Burnham Overy Staithe where he ran the Boathouse for forty-one years. In his 'retirement' he still works on renovating or repairing boats in his Burnham Norton workshop and loves to go out sailing in his boat *Maggie May*.

topper

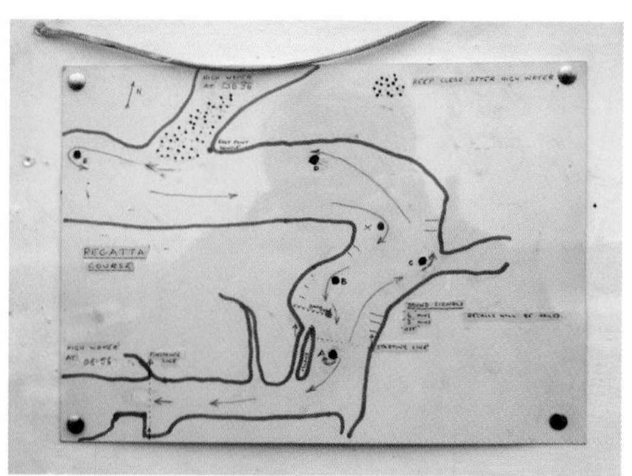

KEEP CLEAR AFTER HIGH WATER
REGATTA COURSE
SOUND SIGNALS
STARTING LINE

171682

FRIDAY 12th August
Ladies Race 6pm
Children's Race (Under 17)
6:05pm
Enter here 5:30pm
ALL WELCOME

Sailing at Burnham Overy Staithe

The Sailing Club and Burnham Overy Regatta were both started before the Second World War. The Regatta always took place in August, along with the Water Sports event. After a break, the Sailing Club was revived in 1961 by a small group including Peter Beck. In recent years the Sailing Club and Burnham Overy Regatta have been amalgamated.

Right, from top
Peter Beck, Robin Anderson with Ellie Jamieson, and Tom Mulholland

Children's races.

Right
Burnham Overy Water Sports originally started in pre-war days. It was discontinued because of insurance concerns before restarting in 2011 and once again offers an afternoon of family fun. The one-man-and-a-dog race is particularly popular.

DUFFEY II

Gun Hill

An excellent walk, starting from Overy Staithe, runs along the sea wall through the marshes, towards the beach at Gun Hill with Scolt Head Island beyond.

Norfolk Coast Path
Burnham Overy Staithe
11/2 m
Norfolk Coast Path
Holkham Gap 2 m
The Hero Bar and
Restaurant 11/2 m
01328 738334

Grey Goose and The Ark

The only two surviving members of the many beach huts which used to be here on the approach to Scolt Head Island.

Coastal Defence Work

The constant battle against the encroaching North Sea continues along the Norfolk coast, as work on these coastal defences shows.

Not coastal army manoeuvres, but attempts to rescue the digger constructing the groynes, which became stuck in the heavy mud of the harbour.

Overy Staithe Windmill

Overy Staithe Mill, built by Edmund Savory in 1816, was donated to the National Trust in 1958 and is now rented out as holiday accommodation.

Overy Watermill

Overy Watermill, like the windmill up the hill, was built by local miller and businessman Edmund Savory in 1790. The houses were built for the mill and farm workers and the complex had its own blacksmith shop.

Mill Corner, Burnham Overy.

NOTICE
FISHING
STRICTLY
PRESERVED

THE NATIONAL TRUST
BURNHAM OVERY
WATER MILL
FOR UPKEEP

MRS. PREEDYS
COTTAGE

PRIVATE
PARKING

Burnham Overy Town

Driving through the small cluster of houses in Overy Town, under the shelter of St Clement's Church, it is hard to imagine that this was once the major port of the Burnhams until the silting of the channel hundreds of years ago.

Left
1953 flood

These statues represent the four seasons and the local story is that they were received in payment for work carried out for the Earl of Leicester. The 1953 photograph opposite shows how the statues were originally arranged in two tiers.

BROTHER
CROSS

·OSTRICH HOUSE·

Sunday Newspapers

Derek and Kathleen Rout sell Sunday newspapers from a shed in their back garden in Burnham Overy Town. They have been doing this for more than thirty-five years.

St Clement's Church, Overy Town

Situated at the top of a small hill, overlooking the surrounding countryside, St Clement's is possibly the most unusual-looking church in the Burnhams. It was originally built in the form of a cross, but there have been many changes over the centuries. The original tower has been shortened and is now topped with an interesting bell turret. The graveyard features some intricately carved headstones.

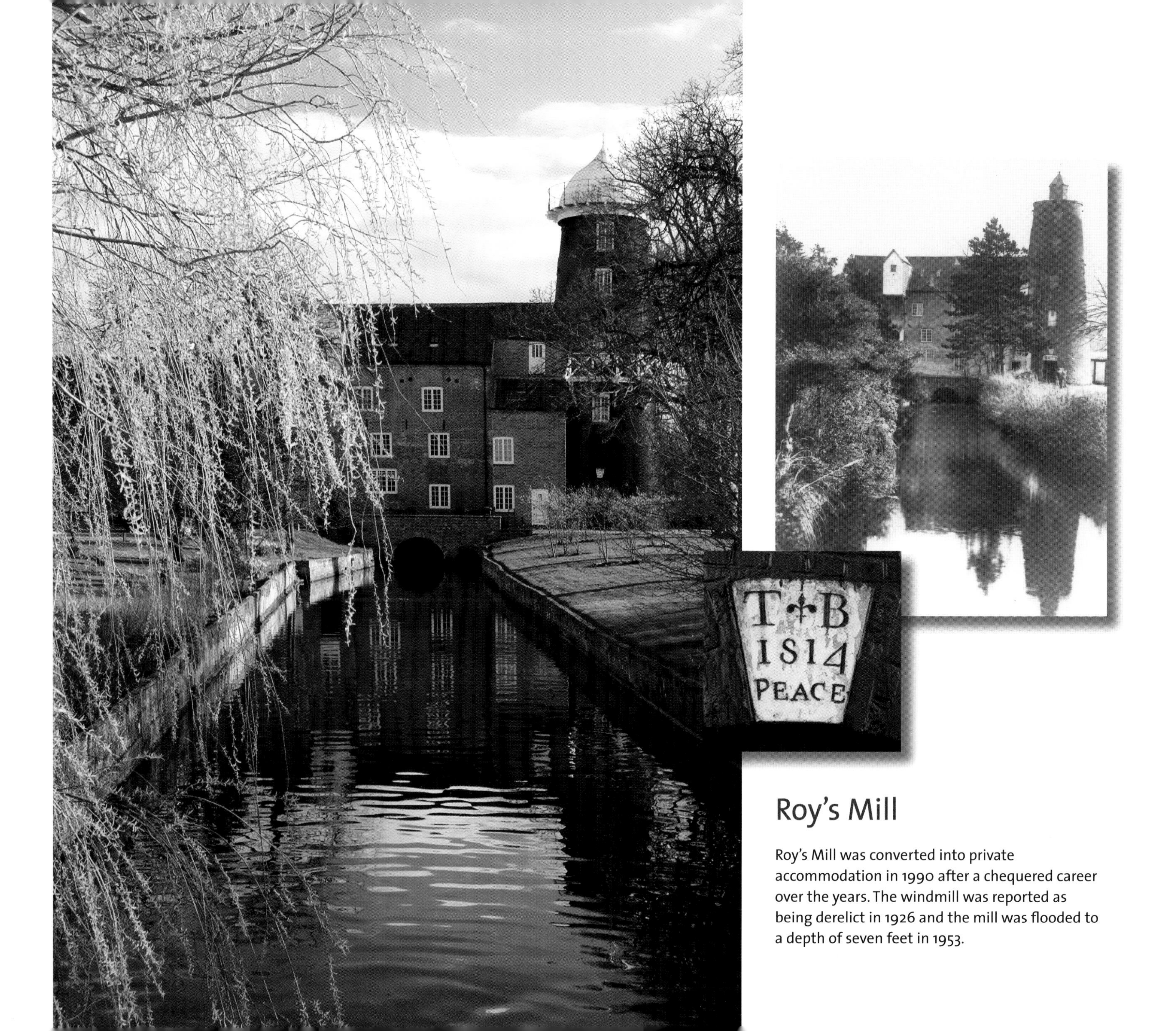

Roy's Mill

Roy's Mill was converted into private accommodation in 1990 after a chequered career over the years. The windmill was reported as being derelict in 1926 and the mill was flooded to a depth of seven feet in 1953.

BY ROAD

BURNHAM THORPE
BIRTHPLACE OF
HORATIO NELSON
29TH SEPTEMBER, 1758.

Burnham Thorpe

Burnham Thorpe is probably best known as the birthplace of England's maritime hero of the Napoleonic Wars, Horatio Nelson, whose father, Edmund, was rector here and at Burnham Norton. Certainly, the village attracts tourists from all over the world who generally drink the admiral's health in the eponymous Lord Nelson pub, itself a shrine to Thorpe's most famous son.

H.M.S.
VICTORY

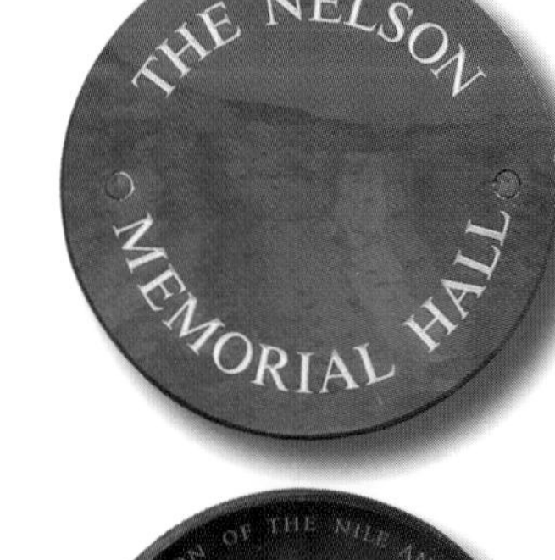
THE NELSON
MEMORIAL HALL

ADMIRAL LORD NELSON OF THE NILE AND BURNHAM THORPE
1758-1805

TO CHURCH
VILLAGE HALL

Cricket Match
(Peter Betjemann Trophy Match)
BURNHAM THORPE AND OTHER PLACES
VS
BURNHAM THORPE AND BEYOND
OUR TEAM OF EXPERIENCED SELECTORS WISH TO MAKE IT CLEAR THAT IF YOU TURN UP YOU WILL BE SELECTED!!
"THE PETER BETJEMANN SHIELD" WILL BE AWARDED TO "THE MOST ENTERTAINING PLAYER"!!
STARTS 1pm
BANK HOLIDAY SUNDAY
28th AUGUST 2011
Teas for non-cricketers - £2 per person (from 4pm)
SORRY DUCK RACE CANCELLED

BURNHAM
THORPE
BOWLS

ROYAL MAIL
E R

THE BIRTHPLACE OF
ADMIRAL LORD NELSON
THE OLD RESTORY IN WHICH THE ADMIRAL WAS BORN,
STOOD TWENTY YARDS BACK FROM THIS WALL
IT WAS PULLED DOWN IN 1803
PRESENTED BY H.M.S. TYNE
FLAGSHIP OF THE
COMMANDER-IN-CHIEF
HOME FLEET
AUGUST 1959

BURNHAM THORPE PARISH COUNCIL
PARISH NOTICE BOARD

W
E

THE FORGE

DO NOT PAR
IN FAR RD

FREE RANGE
BANTAM EGGS
£1.20 DOZEN

PLEASE
PARK
ON
GRASS

DUE TO THEFT OF
EGGS AT WEEKENDS
NO EGGS WILL BE
SOLD ON SATURDAYS
OR SUNDAYS.

30
30

The Lord Nelson

Known as the Plough in Nelson's day and renamed in his honour in 1807, just two years after the battle of Trafalgar, the Lord Nelson is now a much extended pub, serving meals and holding festivals in the grounds during the summer.

Left
The legendary Les Winter, former landlord and Nelson expert.

Below
Nothing and everything has changed since Les's day. Thirty-five years separates these two photographs.

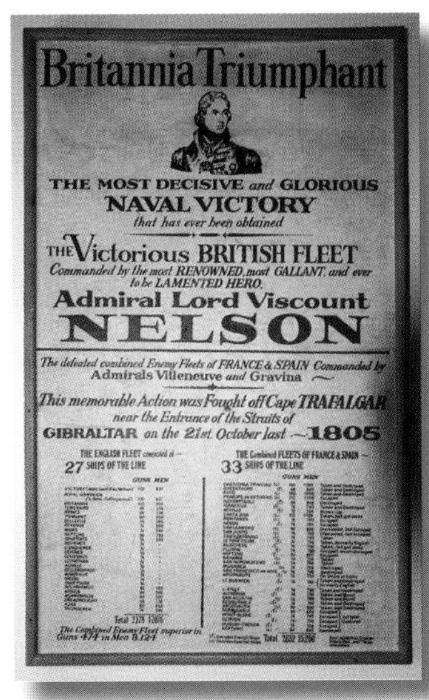

Hazard
Unfenced
Water

THE LORD NELSON
GREENE KING
LARGE BEER GARDEN
&
CHILDREN'S PLAY AREA
The Lord Nelson
NELSON'S LOCAL
Welcome to
Nelson's
Local
Shop.
Open
Nelson's Blood

The King's Morris

Regular sightings of the King's Morris can be had throughout the summer months as they display their athletic dancing skills outside (and sometimes inside) local pubs. Indeed they have the dubious distinction of appearing in all the *People & Places* books published so far!

The Nelson Shanty Men

Chris Jacklin was inspired by the many shantymen groups performing at the Tall Ships race and was helped by the Sheringham Shantymen before founding the Nelson Shantymen in 2010. They are based at the Lord Nelson pub and practice in the Victory Barn. They now sing at various events in the area, entertaining and raising money for charity.

The Leith House Plum Orchard

Nina Plumbe was born in Leith House, Burnham Thorpe. Her father, Garry Maufe, planted the trees between 1976 and 1978. Nina took over in 1992.

The orchard has almost 3,000 plum trees with over thirty-five different varieties, probably the most varied dedicated plum orchard in the country. The plums ripen over a period of about two months from mid July with Hermans, the first variety, until mid September when they finish with Coe's Golden Drop and Anna Spath.

Nina drives a Tuk Tuk, a motorised rickshaw, as she says, for fun, easy parking and local deliveries.

All Saints' Church, Burnham Thorpe

Probably the most visited church in the Burnhams, because of its connections with Horatio Nelson. Burnham Thorpe was Nelson's birthplace and his father was rector of All Saints'. There is a wealth of Nelson memorabilia on display with panels describing his life and famous maritime victories.

All Saints' has much to recommend it in its own right, particularly the famous Calthorpe brass in the chancel depicting the Lancastrian knight, Sir William Calthorpe, who died in 1420.

said that
WALTER
FUTTER
NORFOLKS
OCTR 13TH 1915

S M N
MEMORY · OF · ROBINS: COOK · WHO · DIED · APRIL · 14 · 1881
OF · SOPHIA · HIS · WIFE · WHO · DIED · NOV 21 · 1875

Burnham Deepdale

Burnham Deepdale is strung loosely along the coast road adjacent to Brancaster Staithe. Although St Mary's Church is part of the Saxon Shore benefice which runs as far west as Old Hunstanton, Deepdale has its own identity with a small hub of shops, including a garage and supermarket, based around Deepdale Farms run by Alister and Jason Borthwick, with its camping ground and information centre.

NO UNAUTHORISED
SHOOTING ON
THESE MARSHES
ALLOWED. B.C.R.G.C.

little
giggles
Norfolk's fun and funky toy and gift shop!
www.littlegigglesgifts.co.uk
Gone Crabbing®
www.gonecrabbing.co.uk
Relish
Jewellery
Accessories
Gifts
Deepdale
Information
Activities & Attractions
Guidebooks
Travel Information
Internet Access
Photocopy & Fax
What's On
Backpackers Hostel
Camping
Open
All Year
Tipis
Deepdale Granary
Group Hostel
DEEPDALE GRANARY
40
norfolk
hideaways
Leftley's

murco
Deepdale
Backpackers
This courtyard is ONLY for those staying in the hostel, except for access to the freezers, vending machine and laundry
NO PARKING
Entrance used by heavy farm machinery
Please use car park or layby opposite
DEEPDALE
café
01485 211055
www.deepdalecafe.co.uk
FRESH CRAB
DALEGATE MARKET PE31
BURNHAM DEEPDALE
Shopping & Café
Health and Safety
Please DO NOT enter this courtyard
Thank you

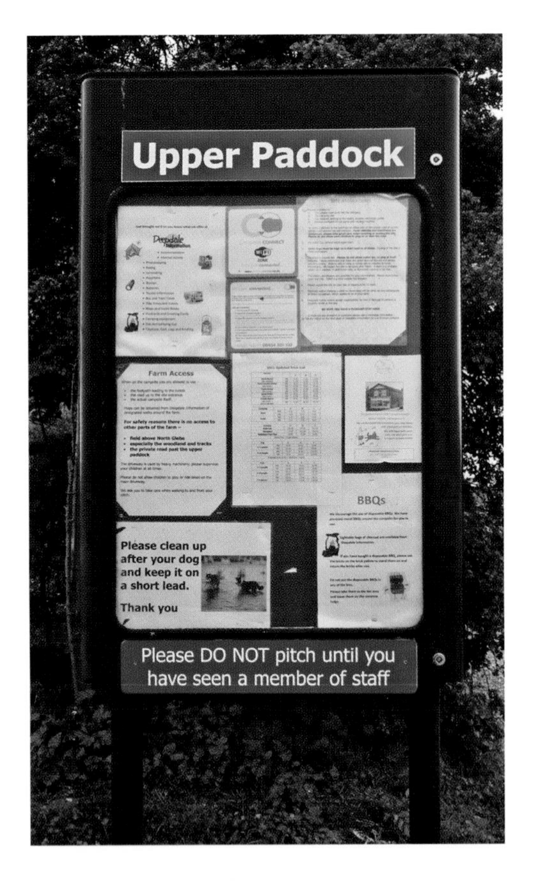
Upper Paddock
Farm Access
BBQs
Please clean up after your dog and keep it on a short lead.
Thank you
Please DO NOT pitch until you have seen a member of staff

Deepdale
Backpackers & Camping
RECEPTION at
Deepdale Information

DEEPDALE
FORGE
5
MPH
Children playing
Please drive slowly

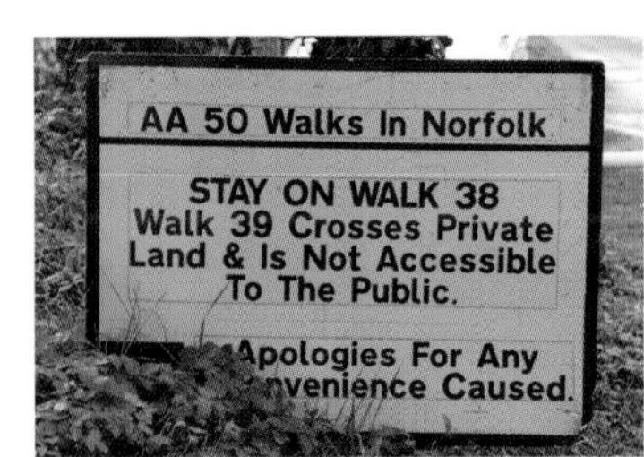
AA 50 Walks In Norfolk
STAY ON WALK 38
Walk 39 Crosses Private Land & Is Not Accessible To The Public.
Apologies For Any
nvenience Caused.

Eggs from these hens are for sale across the road at Deepdale Information.

PRIVATE
COASTAL PATH
100YDS

CAMPING

Saint Mary's Church, Burnham Deepdale

St Mary's contains many fragments of fifteenth-century stained glass, much of which has been identified as the work of the Norwich School, a medieval workshop that turned out characteristic feathery angels and brightly coloured cartoon-like figures. The Sun-and-Moon face in the porch was originally part of a large crucifixion scene, where it signified the darkness that came over the Earth following the death of Christ. In the tower are delightful fragments making a figure of Mary Magdalene and in the north-west window a collection including small roundels of the Trinity and St Ursula.

A German vestment of the 1490s has been preserved on the north wall with woven figures almost as old as the ancient glass.

The Romanesque font is quite stunning. It shows the tasks of each month of the year, which include pruning the vines – obviously Norfolk enjoyed a warmer climate in Norman times than it does today! The font, now raised on a dais, may once have stood on the floor of the church, where it would have been used for adult baptisms.

Deepdale Christmas Fair

The Christmas Fair started in 2008 and now features more than fifty stalls selling local crafts and produce. Brancaster Church of England Children's Choir, Fakenham Town Band and Hunstanton Concert Band provide seasonal music over the weekend. The mulled wine stall (centre) is always very popular

Hare & Hen Pottery

Philippa Lee has been working as a potter, producing domestic ware, since 1976. She opened a new craft shop and pottery, 'the hare and the hen' at Burnham Deepdale in April 2010, where she produces pots in a wonderful light space surrounded by handmade crafts.

Philippa tries to make pots that people want to use and enjoy, and oven dishes that become part of everyday life, with decorations to make people smile.

Burnham Norton

Quietly situated off the main coast road with a splendid church a good mile inland, possibly separated from the village by the effects of the bubonic plague in the fourteenth century, Burnham Norton is an access point for excellent walks across the coastal marshes.

BURNHAM NORTON

TELEPHONE

PROPERTY
TO LET
HOLKHAM ESTATE
TEL: 01328 710227
www.holkham.co.uk

Many years ago, this was a pub serving Bullards' Ales. Burnham Norton no longer has a pub, but the house retains the name 'Prince of Wales'. The bunting in the photograph was to celebrate the Royal Wedding of 2011.

Zeeblik

THE STEP

SEA PEEPS
19

ST. ANTHONY'S COTTAGE
BURNHAM NORTON
PARISH MEETING

CREEK COTTAGE

EASTERN
COUNTIES

Saint Margaret's Church, Burnham Norton

St Margaret's stands alone on the hill overlooking Burnham Norton with superb views over to the marshes and coast. It has a Saxon round tower dating back 1000 years. There is a pre-Reformation 'wine glass' pulpit featuring the early doctors of the church: Ambrose, Augustine, Gregory and Jerome. Horatio Nelson's father was rector here for a time and Captain Woodget, master of the famous clipper *Cutty Sark*, is buried in the chuchyard.

W
R
DIEV ET MON DROIT
1697

Polly Ionides

Polly is a Fellow of the Royal British Society of Sculptors and a member of the Art Workers Guild. She lives and works in north Norfolk although she keeps a studio in London.

She works mostly in stone and bronze, on commissions for private homes and gardens.

Weathervanes

Some of the great variety of weathervanes to be found in the Burnhams. Once you've taken a couple of photos, you're on your way to a collection!

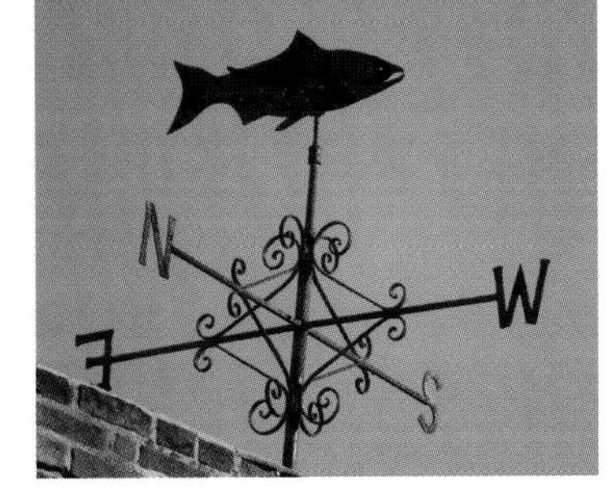

Burnham Norton Parish Walks
Burnham Norton
Burnham Overy Staithe
Burnham Overy Town
Welcome to
Holkham (Burnham Norton)
National Nature Reserve
POLICE
WARNING
DON'T LEAVE
VALUABLES IN
YOUR VEHICLE

BURNHAM'S OVERY& NORTON
WILDFOWLING ASSOCIATION
SHOOTING RIGHTS
STRICTLY RESERVED FOR
MEMBERS OF BONWA
NO UNAUTHORISED SHOOTING
BEWARE SHOOTING IN PROGRESS
SEPTEMBER 1ST TO FEBRUARY 20TH
B.O.N.W.A
HOLKHAM ESTATE

Bibliography

A Dream of the Land – John Hansell

East Anglia Villages – John Potter

The Village Pub – Roger Protz and Homer Sykes

Book of the Burnhams – Halsgrove Press

A Walk around Burnham Market – Burnhams WEA

Acknowledgements

Sean Allen, Robin Anderson, Ben Andrews, Sue Arnold, Brian Baldwin, Ellie Beachell, Peter Beck, Kate Bennett, Janet Betts, Nicky Bond, Charles & Brygida Bourn, Biddie Bunkle, Nod Butcher, Ned Catt, Karen Cole, Harry, Katherine & Mary Cory-Wright, Mick & Carole Coutanche, Anne Cringle, David Crombie, Debbie Davies, Beverley Defew, Diane Eastwood, Sarah Eddison, Sue Elston, Keiron Evennett, Matthew Falvey, Fiona Farrow, Martin Flowerdew, Jo Francis, Nick Fryer, Chris Geering, Annie Gordon, Maxwell & Vicky Graham-Wood, James Granger, Steve, Sheila & Tony Green, James Groom, Veronica Groom, Mike Gurney, Robert Harker, Ian Heighton and the King's Morris, Brian Hetherington, Clifford & Kevin Hewitt, Lynn Hinson, Rev. Graham Hitchins, Anna Holman, Arthur Howell, Gloria Hurn, Polly Ionides, Chris Jacklin, Ellie Jamieson, Rob & Julie King, Debbie Lawton, Philippa and Helen Lee, Brian Lynn, Teresa Mahon, Trevor Manning, John Middleton; Geoff Misson, Tom Mulholland, Rev. Kim Nally, Charlie Neale, Pamela Noyes, Joan Nudds, Bill Offord, Nina Plumbe, Enid Poll, Terry Rand, Ann Randall, Scott Raven, Brian Rix, Simon Rix, Gary Robins, Jenny Rose, Derek & Kathleen Rout, Andrew Ruffhead, Rob Rutterford, Andrea St Quintin, Ivan Sands, Sabine Schmitt, Juliette Short, Dave, Jack & Robert Smith, Dorothy Smith, Sophie Smith, Alastair Steele, Brian Symonds; Emma Tagg, Kenny Thompson, Pam Thompson, Sam Turner, Alan & Vicky Utting, John Utting, Joanna Warner, Lillie Webster, Rev. Christopher Wood, Jeanne Whittome, Steven Willsher, Sally Wordingham.

Particular thanks to Rev. Christopher Wood for writing the notes on Deepdale Church and the Carmelite Friary.

Photo Credits

Many thanks to Enid Poll for the photo of the Friary on page 27, Ashley Rix for the photos on page 50, to Des Barkes for the photos on page 52, Keiron Tuvell for the photos on page 84, Alex Christie for the photos on page 122, Joan Nudds for the photo of Burnham Overy Town floods on page 134 and to Homer Sykes for the photo of Les Winter on page 153. Thanks also to Carole Coutanche for the DUKW photo on page 105.

Finally, many thanks to Sarah Eddison for her help and encouragement throughout.

The Authors

Hazel Denslow was born in Essex, spent most of her married life in Hertfordshire and moved to Norfolk in 1993. Having attended Photoshop sessions in Wells Library in 2004, she moved on to learning how to use a digital camera and from there completed a three years NCFE course in Digital Photography. She has two daughters, one son and eight grandchildren.

John Warham retired from a business career working in Asia, before moving to Norfolk, and is amazed to find himself completing a third book in the *People & Places* series. John lives in Thornham, which was the first subject in this series, and studied digital photography at Wells for five years. He is married to Sue and they have two grownup children and a granddaughter.

Dick Malt has designed all the books in this series and is the unsung hero of the project. His wise counsel and critical advice have helped the authors to avoid many potential catastrophes. Dick lives in Hoe with his wife Sue. This book is as much his as ours.

Photographic Notes

Except where otherwise stated, all the photos in this book were taken by John Warham and Hazel Denslow between 2010 and 2012. John uses Canon 450D and 50D digital camera bodies with Canon EF70-300mm DO IS USM, Canon EFS 17-85mmIS and Sigma 10-20mm lenses. Hazel uses a Panasonic Lumix DMC-G1K digital camera with a 14-45 mm/F3.5-5.6 ASPH./MEGA O.I.S lens and a 45-200 mm/F4.0-5.6 MEGA O.I.S lens. In addition she uses a Panasonic Lumix DMC-FS 10. The photographs were produced using Adobe Photoshop CS4 and Elements 7.